A gift for:

_____

From:

_____

LITTLE BLACK GIRL

Written By

Brittany Green

Illustrations By

Fuuji Takashi

Michelle Obama: Lawyer, Author and Former First African American First Lady of the United States and first First Lady to attend an Ivy League university.

Madame CJ Walker: Born in 1867, Sarah Breedlove, was the first black women to become a millionaire in America after developing her own successful hair care line.

Simone Manuel: An American competition swimmer, Simone won 2 gold and 2 silver medals at the 2016 Olympics in Rio. Simone became the first African American woman to win the gold medal for individual swimming setting both Olympic and American records.

Oprah: Media Mogul, Actress, Producer, Talk show host, Philanthropist, and the richest African American in the world.

Shonda Rhimes: Author, Producer and Creator of television shows such as Grey's Anatomy, How to Get Away with Murder and Scandal.

SUMMARY

Queen Amina or Queen Aminatu: A fierce militant strategist and Queen of what is now the north center region of Nigeria in the 1500's.

Queen Mekeda: Also known as the Queen of Sheba, Mekada was Queen in Ethiopia around 960 B.C. Mentions of Queen Makeda can be found in both the Koran and the Bible.

Queen Nefertiti: Queen of Egypt in the 1350's B.C. Known for starting a religious revolution for serving only one God.

Mary, Katherine and Dorothy: Three female mathematicians who aided in assisting the first American being put into orbit. Their story was told in the 2017 film Hidden Figures.

Beyonce: American singer, dancer, songwriter, actress with more than 100 million albums sold and 22 Grammys.

And never think of yourself as secondary or less because beautiful black girl, you are more wonderful than words can express.

You are one of a kind, so always be you.
Be a light in this world, let your heart shine through.

You are so wanted.
You are cherished.
You are so divine.
You are worthy.

You are precious.
Your beauty transcends
space and time.

So please little black girl, always remember who you are. Trust in the Lord because with his guidance I know you will go far.

You can pave your own way and bypass the back of the line.

You can own your own television network like Oprah.
You could write the stories like Shonda Rhimes.

You can do hair like
Madam CJ Walker.
You can swim like
Simone Manuel.

You can sing tunes like Beyonce.
You could be First Lady like Michelle.

Your possibilities are limitless there's nothing you can't do. Mary, Katherine and Dorothy already showed you your mind can take you to the Moon.

You are a descendant of Queens, their blood flows through your veins.
They may not teach you in school, but please remember these names
Amina, Makeda, and Nefertiti are all queens that looked like you. And
because you are their descendant that means you're royalty too!

You come from a group exclusive and proud.
A group that can't help but stand out in a crowd.

Do you know that your hair, so thick and curly, doesn't need to be straightened so that you can feel worthy?

Do you know that your skin, so golden honey brown, reflects your inner strength that can never be broken down?

Little Black Girl, do you know who you are?
Do you know that your smile shines bright as the stars?

This book is dedicated to my daughter Zhayria Jeaveh Tillman. You are the most precious gift I could ever receive. I am so proud to be your mommy. I hope you enjoy this book as it is my love letter to you.

Special thanks to all that encouraged me to publish this book. This would not have happened without your support!

You are a mountain.
You come from mountains.
You are not a pile of spaghetti.

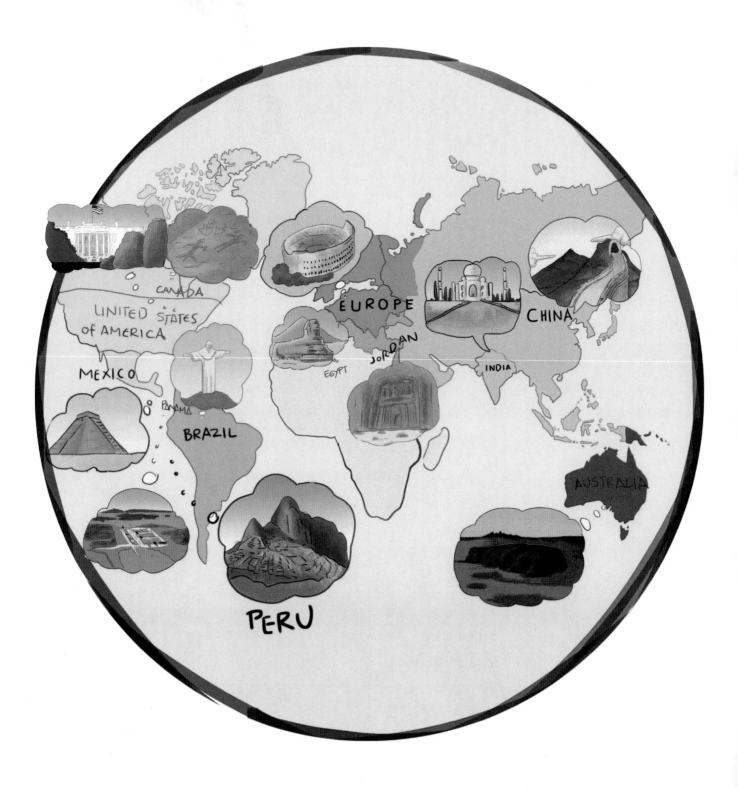

Little Mountain, I'm so grateful that your ancestors built cities and countries, and contributed so much to help us live the lives we lead today.

Most importantly, I'm grateful they were strong enough to live through difficult times so that you could eventually be born.

Never forget who you came from. Never forget who you are, Little Mountain.

Believe no lies.

Author's Note to Caregivers

This book is written as an introduction to the concept of racism. I intentionally avoided delving into specific examples of overt racism, institutional racism, and inequality to allow caregivers to introduce these heavier concepts to their child at the right time for their family, taking their child's sensitivities and phase of development into account.

As you read this book with your child, please insert your values, interpretations, and experiences to help your child connect with the book in a more personal way. Here are a few questions you may want to ask your child as you read this book, to help deepen their understanding and facilitate discussion:

- What words would you use to describe yourself?
- Can you tell me about the people you come from known as your ancestors?
- How would you feel if someone told you that you are not as important as they are? Would you believe them? What would you say to them?
- What if you heard someone say that light or white skin was better? Would you believe them? What would you say to them?
- What if you hear someone tell your friend that they are not as good or as important because they come from India or from China or from Guatemala? Would you believe them? Do you think your friend might believe them? How can you help your friend to know what is a lie and what is the truth? What would you tell your friend?

For Further Reading:

- *All the Colors We Are,* by Katie Kissinger
- *Whoever You Are,* by Mem Fox
- *Anti-Racism for Kids: A Quick and Simple Guide for Parents to Teach Their Children About Equality, Diversity, Inclusion, and Deal With Prejudice and Discrimination in Daily Life Situations,* by Tiffany Brown
- *Race Cars: A children's book about white privilege,* by Jenny Devenny
- *Something Happened in Our Town: A Child's Story About Racial Injustice,* by Marianne Celano, PhD and Marietta Collins, PhD

Made in the USA
Las Vegas, NV
01 February 2021